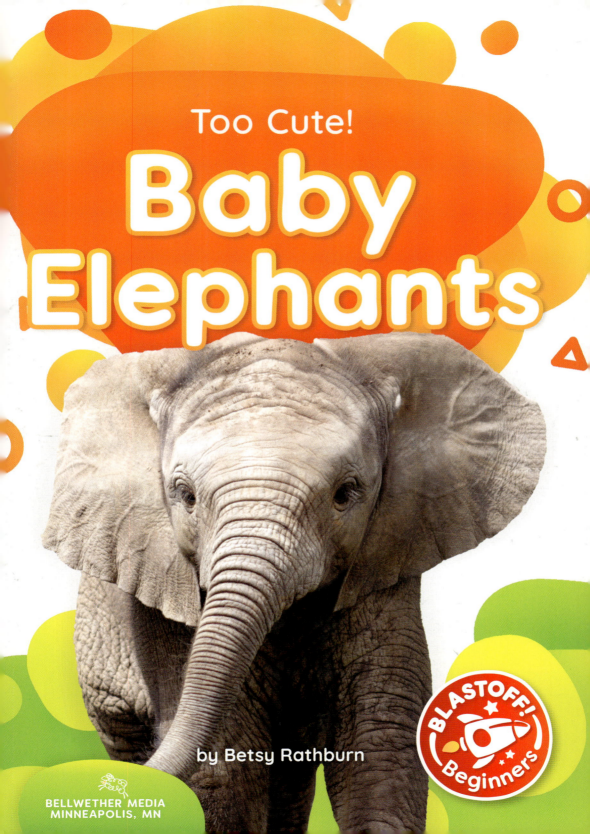

Blastoff! Beginners are developed by literacy experts and educators to meet the needs of early readers. These engaging informational texts support young children as they begin reading about their world. Through simple language and high frequency words paired with crisp, colorful photos, Blastoff! Beginners launch young readers into the universe of independent reading.

Sight Words in This Book

a	eat	look	their
and	for	other	they
are	get	play	to
at	her	run	up
big	is	some	use
by	long	the	with

This edition first published in 2024 by Bellwether Media, Inc.

No part of this publication may be reproduced in whole or in part without written permission of the publisher. For information regarding permission, write to Bellwether Media, Inc., Attention: Permissions Department, 6012 Blue Circle Drive, Minnetonka, MN 55343.

Library of Congress Cataloging-in-Publication Data

Names: Rathburn, Betsy, author.
Title: Baby elephants / by Betsy Rathburn.
Description: Minneapolis, MN : Bellwether Media, Inc., 2024. | Series: Blastoff! Beginners. Too cute! | Includes bibliographical references and index. | Audience: Ages PreK-2 | Audience: Grades K-1
Identifiers: LCCN 2023000125 | ISBN 9798886874044 (library binding) | ISBN 9798886875928 (ebook)
Subjects: LCSH: Elephants--Infancy--Juvenile literature.
Classification: LCC QL737.P98 R37 2024 | DDC 599.6713/92--dc23/eng/20230105
LC record available at https://lccn.loc.gov/2023000125

Text copyright © 2024 by Bellwether Media, Inc. BLASTOFF! BEGINNERS and associated logos are trademarks and/or registered trademarks of Bellwether Media, Inc.

Editor: Rachael Barnes   Designer: Laura Sowers

Printed in the United States of America, North Mankato, MN.

Table of Contents

A Baby Elephant!	4
Herd Life	6
Growing Up!	16
Baby Elephant Facts	22
Glossary	23
To Learn More	24
Index	24

A Baby Elephant!

Look at the baby elephant.
Hello, calf!

Herd Life

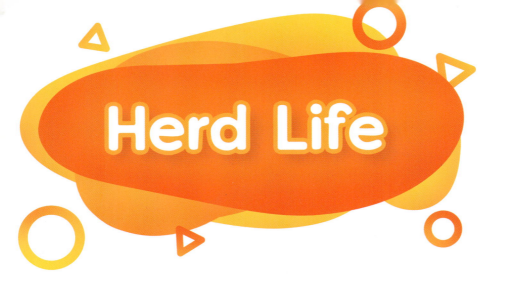

Calves are big babies! They travel with their **herd**.

herd

They stay by mom. They hold her tail.

They drink
mom's milk.
They drink a lot!

They pick up plants to eat. They use their **trunk**.

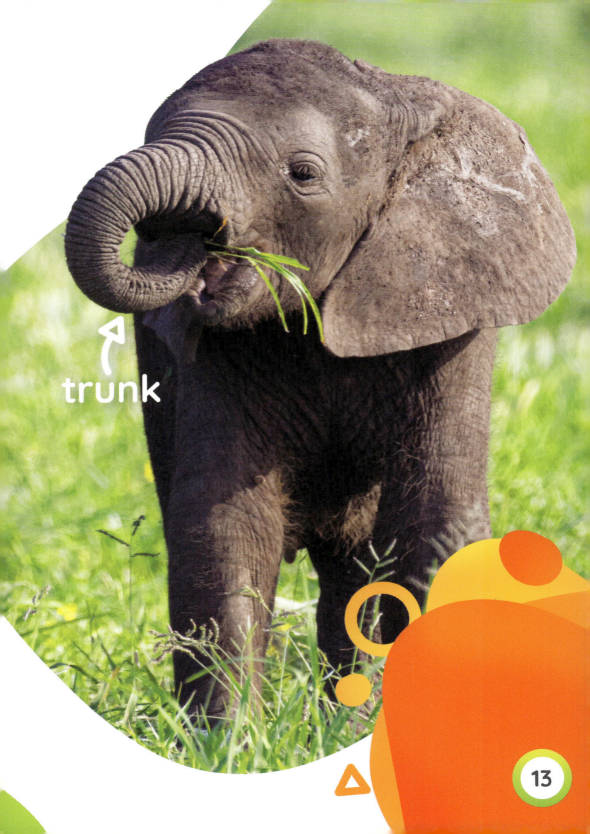

They play with their herd. They **trumpet** and run!

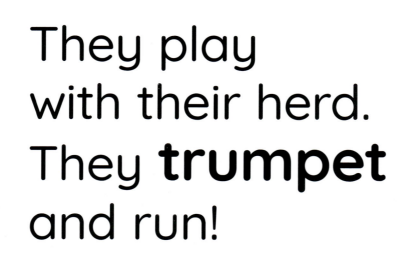

trumpeting

Growing Up!

Calves get huge! They grow long **tusks**.

tusk

They stay
with mom
for years.

Some leave mom.
Others stay.
The herd
is family!

Baby Elephant Facts

Elephant Life Stages

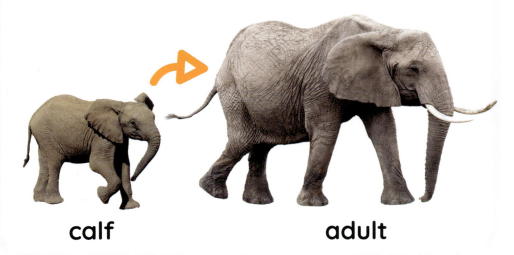

calf   adult

A Day in the Life

drink mom's milk   eat plants   trumpet

Glossary

herd
a group of elephants

trumpet
to make a horn sound with a trunk

trunk
the long nose and upper lip of an elephant

tusks
long teeth

To Learn More

ON THE WEB

FACTSURFER

Factsurfer.com gives you a safe, fun way to find more information.

1. Go to www.factsurfer.com.

2. Enter "baby elephants" into the search box and click 🔍.

3. Select your book cover to see a list of related content.

Index

drink, 10, 11	mom, 8, 9, 10, 18, 20	trunk, 12, 13
eat, 12	plants, 12	tusks, 16
elephant, 4	play, 14	
family, 20	run, 14	
grow, 16	tail, 8	
herd, 6, 7, 14, 20	travel, 6	
milk, 10, 11	trumpet, 14, 15	

The images in this book are reproduced through the courtesy of: JONATHAN PLEDGER, cover, pp. 6, 18-19; THRUZ PANYAWACHIROPAS, pp. 3, 5; FeelplusCreator, p. 4; slowmotiongli, pp. 6-7; FrentaN, p. 8; 1001slide, pp. 8-9; Barbara Ash, pp. 10-11; Sandra Clayton, pp. 12-13; Gunter Nuyts, p. 14; Mark Levy/ Alamy, pp. 14-15; Bkamprath, p. 16; manfredstutz, pp. 16-17; Independent birds, p. 20; CherylRamalho, pp. 20-21; Rich Carey, p. 22 (calf); GoodFocused, p. 22 (adult); Dietmar Rauscher, p. 22 (drink mom's milk); Marcin Osman, p. 22 (eat plants); Stefan W. Moeller, p. 22 (trumpet); paula french, p. 23 (herd); Jane Rix, p. 23 (trumpet); Nataliya Hora, p. 23 (trunk); Ilyas Kalimullin, p. 23 (tusks).